Copyright © 2017 by Alan D. Rice

Published under permission in Nigeria by:

Kings Media Limited
1, Tanimola Street, Ijebu-Ode
Ogun State, Nigeria

No part of this publication may be reproduced or transmitted in any form by any means, electronic or mechanical, including photocopying, recording, or by any information storage and retrieval system, without prior written permission from the author.

FOR SALE IN NIGERIA ONLY

TABLE OF CONTENTS

1. *A SHORT DESCRIPTION OF FOREX*
2. *PSYCHOLOGY OF TRADING*
3. *FUNDAMENTAL VERSUS TECHNICAL TRADING STYLES*
4. *GETTING TO KNOW THE CURRENCIES*
5. TECHNICAL CHARTS
6. SUPPORT AND RESISTANCE TRENDS
7. BREAKOUT TRENDS
8. CANDLESTICK CHARTS
9. RISK MANAGEMENT AND ORDER PROTECTION
10. CONCLUSION

CHAPTER 1:

A SHORT DESCRIPTION OF FOREX

Forex, currency trading, FX, and foreign exchange trading are all words used to talk about a $5.3 trillion per day trading market. The foreign exchange market is an exchange of one countries money for another, at an agreed upon exchange rate.

When you trade in the FX market, you trade in a decentralized global market, where you speculate about which currency will perform better or worse against another currency.

There are a couple of keywords you should learn.
Decentralized market: this type of market is set up to have various networks, without a centralized location. The stock exchange has centralized places throughout the world. The New York Stock Exchange
or NYSE is a centralized market for the USA and companies. Companies worldwide can get listed on the NYSE or list on their countries market. The LSE or London Stock Exchange is another location that regulates how stocks trade on the open market and the price. The forex market has several players, with regulation, but no central location. The FX market dealers can list competing rates, whereas the stock price for a company is the only quote you will ever see listed through any broker.

Speculate: speculation is about trading currency for a profitable return, but with a risk of loss. Speculators during the gold rush would find a plot of land, hope it would yield gold, and many ended up
losing everything. Forex can be similar. You find a currency to invest in for a set period, hoping for a gain, but may lose. In 2010, a study determined that only 33 percent of currency traders were profitable.

History of Forex

Trading currency is not a new concept, but the market has evolved over time. The world started with a barter process. One person would see value in something another individual had and trade something they owned to get what they wanted. Of course, the other person needed to see the value in what the first individual offered for the trade.

As far back as 15,000 BCE, goods were used as "currency" to barter. Grain and cattle were the first money used. Commodity money appeared in 3000 BC when places like Mesopotamia and China started using shells as money to trade for goods. China started using bronze in the shape of knives and spades in 1000 BC. Money became bronze for products made by India and China, eventually stamped with insignias to symbolize the country of origin.

Paper money in the form of IOUs came next. As long as there was value found in an object like bronze, gold, or silver, it was money to trade for handmade goods. Eventually, the world decided it was better to form regulated currency, with particular designs to show the country of origin and to set a rate of exchange.

People realized they could exchange their bronze, gold, or silver for another country's gaining or losing in the trade based on the purity of the metal used. The gold and other currency needed to be protected or backed by something of value. Paper money had no real value unless there was something to support it, such as gold. Gold was also a limited metal. It is hard to find, and not enough existed for everyone to use it in trade.

The *gold standard* may be something you have heard about in your other trading experience. A country would back its paper money with gold. A fixed price for gold was set for those who wanted to buy or sell gold, the price then determined the value of the currency. If gold was $500 per ounce, it meant the value of the dollar was 1/500th of an ounce of gold.

Countries abandoned the gold standard after a while. Britain stopped using it after the first World War, and the US finally changed to a new system in 1971. Today, the forex market works on a fiat system. Each country has a currency that is "legal tender," meaning it is used to purchase goods or services. Supply and demand determine the value of money. The more demand for currency, with a limited supply, the more value it has. Gold is valuable because it is a financial asset for central banks and countries. Banks can hedge against loans for their government using gold.

Today, when we say we are trading currency, we mean we are using dealers to earn a profit on the value of one currency against another. Forex traders are not going to their local bank, exchanging their domestic currency for foreign currency or vice versa.

It is one way to trade currency, but the method is better for travelers, who are not looking at the price of money for investment. When you travel to another country, you need to use their currency. Once you are back home, you need to go back to your monetary units.

What Can You Trade

Obviously, forex is an exchange, but not a physical one. You will never hold 1 million of another currency in your hands when you place a trade. Everything is conducted electronically. What you trade is the value of money, versus the actual product.

If you buy EUR/USD, you are trading on the value of the currency on that specific day. You may see a quote online that states: EUR/USD=1.08145. What does this mean? You are trading currency pairs, so if you buy Euros using US dollars, then you need to know what the value of the EUR versus the USD is. The EUR or euro is the base currency, which has a value of 1. The second currency can be the quote or counter currency depending on the broker/dealer. The quote currency will fluctuate and shows you the potential profit you can earn. For example, if you buy in at 1.08145 and sell at 1.08245, there is a change of 100.

But what does this change mean to you? If you do not understand this fundamental principle, it will be difficult to use trading strategies to make a profit. If you have one dollar and eight cents in US currency and you receive 1 euro, which currency is weaker?

If you said the USD, then you are right. It takes more USD to make one euro. If the USD quote is 0.99, then the USD would be more valuable than the euro because you need less than a dollar to make one euro.

Think of it in terms of how far your money can go. If your money can go farther, gain you more in a different currency, then your money has more value because you use less of it to gain more in a different currency.

Now, when you trade in forex, the profit is found in "pips." A pip is 0.0001 in value. A change of 100 is 0.0100 or 100 pips. If you open a trade expecting the quote currency to increase instead of decrease, and it changes 100 pips in an increase, then you make money.

When you select "buy," you are expecting the quote currency to increase in numbers. You expect the number to go from 1.08145 to 1.08146 or higher. Yes, in value against the EUR, the USD is weakening, but remember on a chart, when a number increases from 5 to 6, it is going up. If the number goes from 5 to 4, then it is decreasing. You want the value of the EUR to increase when you buy it and sell USD. You want the EUR value to fall if you sell the EUR and buy USD.

It sounds confusing, and it can be. If you focus on needing an uptrend when you select buy and a downtrend when to sell, then you will be alright. You do not want to stake your strategy on that thought alone, but for this chapter, understand that you buy to take advantage of an uptrend and sell to earn on a down trend.

Why Trade Forex Instead of Stocks

1. The Forex market deals in over $5 trillion per day.

2. It is a 24-hour market, nearly seven days a week.

3. Billion dollar trades can be made, without the market moving significantly.

4. The volume, liquidity, and volatility make it possible to turn a profit.
   In the stock market, you need someone to be interested in buying or selling a company's stock for it to change in price. You can go months without a significant profit when you trade in the stock market.
However, in the forex market, companies, countries, billionaires, millionaires, and retail traders are active.

Countries need to exchange currency for paying for products or services. Businesses that buy products need to exchange their currency for the foreign currency to pay for the goods. Retail traders, whether they are day traders or long-term traders, buy and sell based on dealer quotes for the day to make a profit. In short, the activity is in the forex market, where even the little guy can make a profit.

Beginner Strategy

You have barely touched on how the market works; however, you might have read currency trading books that outlined what the market is, how it works, and you are ready for an investment strategy to turn a profit.
1. Stick with the major currency pairs.
2. Follow the seven pairs for a week.
3. Write in a journal every day about the seven currency pairs. What pairs were up or down?
How significant was the change in the pips?
4. What factors influenced the currency pairs?
5. Repeat steps 1 through 4 every day you invest.

This strategy may not involve investing. You might look at it as nothing more than a silly outline, but this routine matters. Do you think the 33 percent of successful traders get up, look at the quotes, and decide to spend money? No, they know what happened the day before, the week before, the year before.

They know how a currency reacts to certain situations, news, and traders. These top investors, who are highly successful leave nothing to chance. They learned the market, how to read it and understand it. You have to start somewhere.

CHAPTER 2
Psychology of Trading

Trading is risky whether you trade in the stock market, bonds, hedge funds, mutual funds, or the forex market. You can protect yourself against many of the risks if you understand the psychology of trading. The wrong trading psychology can bring you misery and break the bank. You do not want that. You want to be confident in the trades you place, and understand that sometimes losses do occur.

Companies, billionaire traders, and all retail traders suffer loss; how much you lose will depend on whether you make mistakes. A company tries to exchange their currency when it is of better value to them, but this cannot happen all the time. For example, if the domestic currency is valued lower than the foreign exchange, some companies try to pay in their currency rather than trading for the foreign currency where the seller lives. The seller wants their currency to be of more value, so they do not lose out on their earnings.

When a currency is of lower value, the exchange results in less of the trade money. It is disadvantageous, but many companies account for this in some way to minimize the losses, when dealing with imports and exports.

The key lesson is that a company understands there may be a loss when a currency exchange is needed to pay for goods. The business still runs smoothly, and there are no emotions involved because the loss is expected to occur in a company. A company expects to see a variation in sales, which can be a loss one month in money and an increase the next month.

As an individual retail trader in the forex market, you want to be as withdrawn from emotion as a business is. In fact, you should treat your forex trades like a company transaction. You assess the situation, make a plan, and protect your investment strategy. To do otherwise will lead to losses.

Trading Psychology Defined

Trading psychology is a mental and emotional state that will determine your wins and losses in the forex market. You will need to develop certain traits to succeed trading currency.
The top traders know their limits and do not over trade. They set risk management strategies to prevent losing capital. These traders maintain discipline at all times, ensuring they stick to their trading plan. They also know the different between following the herd and not fighting a trend.

11 Things to Avoid and Build a Better Trading Psychology

1. **Trade paralysis**: when you start out as a beginner there is a lot to learn. In the last chapter, you were asked to continue learning and to get to know the top seven currency pairs. There will come a point in your education where you will know everything you can about these pairs. You will start to see patterns, how the news affects the rates, and which brokers offer the best rates.
Soaking up information is great, but you do not want to enter analysis paralysis.

Trade analysis paralysis is when you continue to analyze the market, currency pairs, and never actually place a trade. If you do place a trade, then you may wait in agony to see your losses because you are so sure it will be a loss. Do not let your fear keep you from placing a trade.

2. Yes, there are patterns in the technical analysis you will come to recognize. However, you must also understand that sometimes the market is just random. It may not work as you believe it will, even from months of analysis. These "random" factors can sometimes be seen right before a trade. It lies in the fundamentals, such as a terrorist attack that has everyone pulling back instead of investing. The other random factors are you and traders like you.

You cannot know what other traders are going to do and whether they will try to turn a trend in their favor. One person may not make a wave, but a herd of people following someone else's trend can change the price against you. To account for random events in forex trading, you need to cut emotional ties to the trade, analyze possible outcomes, and place your risk management strategy accordingly.

3. Do not look for more tips. Tips are great when you can trust the person giving them. Unfortunately, anyone can start a blog, try to sell information, and tell you they have the secret formula for currency trading. The truth is—everyone has a different level of risk, starting capital, and goal for their money. When you start to listen to someone else's strategy, and you try to adapt it to fit your needs—you will lose.

4. Check your equity curve. Your equity curve shows your pattern over time. It will help you see if you are gaining a consistent amount of returns or if you are creating your pattern of losses and gains. Checking your equity curve is about analyzing your trading system by more than just the individual trades. Yes, you do need to go over all trades to see what you could do better or what you did right. Journal the information. However, do not get lost on the individual deals that you miss the big picture.

5. When should you take profits? Do you remain in a trade simply because the currency price had a breakout from a trend? There are a time and place to make your profit, but also minimize your loss. You will learn about orders later that will help you set up an appropriate strategy. Then, you will understand that you should take profits at certain points, but also cut your losses.

6. To trade in the currency market, you have to accept the risk. The concept goes back to the orders you can set. You can protect your position, and cut your losses. However, until you take the risk, you will worry about the market fluctuations. Currency prices are going to fluctuate.
You will set your risk as you outline a trading plan, and then you will let the trade play out.

You should accept the risk and not second guess yourself or the market. The market can move because others are getting in and out of it, but that does not mean your position is in trouble.

7. Set alerts to account for proper trading psychology. You can set alerts to certain patterns, news reports, and other market factors. These emails will tell you when something is edging towards meaningful patterns you will trade on for profit. You still do your due diligence by checking the setup for entry to see if it fits within your trading plan and risk aversion.

8. You need to admit when you are wrong. If you cannot recognize when you have placed a trade that was incorrect, then the same thing will continue to happen over and over again. You have to understand that you cannot always get the market right. There are times when you can do everything and be wrong about how the market will react. If you can think of the market regarding percent of profit over time, then you can see your way to making a consistent profit.

9. The market is limitless, but there are also times when you do not want to invest. Certain factors can make the market unsteady, and bigger losses will result. If you look at steady gains over time, versus significant gains, then you may find more to invest in, but never think you have to continue. Yes, the market is limitless in how it will react and how you can place trades, but only your system and risk aversion level can determine if you can handle the various trading options.

10. A trading journal is a must to alleviate negative trading psychology, such as greed, fear, and hesitancy. A trading journal helps you review individual trades, as well as plot your equity curve.

11. As a bonus, you also need to be careful of happiness. Yes, it seems strange to say it, but you can do just as much damage to your capital by being overly happy and excited. There are times when you will place a trade and make a killing. You will want to turn right around and make just as much profit in the next trade. Unfortunately, life doesn't always work favorably for you.

If you always go after the happy feeling, you will lose more than you win. Trading psychology is all about keeping your emotions in check. If you can accept that you will have some losses, gains, and there is a need to treat forex trading as a business, then you will succeed. You may not make millions. You may have a trade that doubles your investment capital. However, you cannot let your emotions cloud your trading plan.

Trading Plan Strategy

The word "strategy" may be used, but in actuality, you should always make a trading scheme—no matter what! A trading plan is a system for how you will trade based on the current market factors and risk aversion level.

The trading plan consists of a few parts:
- Time
- Currency pair
- Trade rationale
- Risk appetite

Forex trades are shorter than stock trades. However, you can try to capture significant shifts in currency prices over several weeks if you want. Most people do not invest in long-term FX trades because the market is open nearly seven days a week. The market opens in New Zealand, just as the USA market is closing. As the world awakens, new markets open, with some hours of overlap, before all that is left is the USA market. Japan wakes up to see what has changed overnight and plans their trades based on Asian financial moves and closing technical patterns from the USA. You could go to sleep and close your position due to market movements around the world before you wake up. So, choose which market you will study and how long you want to be in the trade.

The currency pair will help you figure out the timing, but it is also an essential part of the trading plan.

You have to decide which currency pairs look the best for possible profit. As a beginner, start with the G7 or major currency pairs, then branch out into the G20, as you become more advanced with trading in the forex market.

The trade rationale is whether you are more of a fundamental or technical trader. Are you going to be a trend follower or someone who looks for breakout patterns? Do you want to watch the news and try to predict how the market will react to individual reports? Choosing to be both fundamental and technical to view the global picture is the best way to start analyzing the market. However, you will need to pick a trend or news report to follow to make a profit based on the day's market performance.

The risk appetite is your aversion level. What are you prepared to risk, when it comes to your capital? What are your profit expectations for the trade? Some people assign a risk of 1% to their plan, while others cannot set tight stops because it would mean an immediate sale.

After you research the four factors above, it is time to establish three things:
1. When you will enter the trade
2. The stop loss order
3. The exit point

Entering the trade is about making sure the market is moving in the right direction for your strategy to turn a profit. There are different orders you can use to enter the market, which you will need to learn about as you study forex.
To protect your capital and minimize your risk, you will need some type of stop loss, trailing stop loss, or taking profit order. This order ensures you cut your losses if the market turns against you and allows you to make a profit when it goes with your current position.

Lastly, the automatic orders are your exit point. You may ride a breakout to the top and have a trailing stop loss that closes your position. You may close out early if you have a stop loss that is triggered by market changes. If you are riding the pattern for a profit, then you will have a taking profit order that ensures the sale of the currency at a certain point, keeping the profit you have made, but not trying to get more.

Sometimes experts on the news, on news websites, or in newspapers will say a currency pair should reach x point. Perhaps, they expect a gain of 100 pips. You decide you are happy if the profit is 80 pips, so you set your position to exit at 80 pips profit. The market experts were wrong because of an unforeseen change in the market; you sold at the height of the profit and those who tried to catch the 100 pips without proper exit strategy lost.

From the example, you can tell why it is imperative that you have a plan and stick to it. Yes, if you find you are losing capital because the market moves against you, then sell out. Triggering the stop loss happens when the price hits a particular number. However, you cannot be disappointed or angry at the market if you sold out just before the market turned in your favor. The reason you set a trading plan is to avoid emotions. It ensures you follow through with the plan, accept the losses, learn from your mistakes, and keep trading for profit.

Never enter the forex market without a trading plan as part of your strategy. As you go through the rest of the book, you are going to learn about fundamental and technical strategies. You may want to use the strategies in this book. You can also develop your own from the information you learn, so the strategies better fit your trading style. The point is, those trade rationale strategies work within your overall trading plan.

CHAPTER 3
Fundamental vs. Technical Trading Styles

The currency has two sides. One side is heads, and the other is tails. Paper money has a back and front. You trade two currencies. It might seem silly to think of it like this, but trading has two sides too—albeit, we refer to them as two types of analysis. Both sides of the coins or paper money make the currency complete. It is just like you cannot trade one currency; you must trade it for something. You should not trade with just fundamental or just technical analysis. You should combine both to trade correctly.

Yes, there are times when technical or fundamental information will serve you better. However, if you do not look at the whole picture first, then you may miss an important element. Once you get used to the market, what makes it move, and who the players are—you will be able to go through your analysis quicker and with better results.

Think of trading analysis as a pyramid. You start out with a broad base to support your trading style. You gather information as a building block before you move to the next layer until eventually; you pinpoint a trend, piece of news, or herd of traders that will be lucrative for that moment you want to trade.

Fundamental Analysis

Fundamental analysis is economic, financial, and government information examined to decide how the currency price may move on any given day. You want to ask some key questions:

1. How can I profit from currency movements?
2. What drives the prices?
3. Who drives the prices?
4. What are the personalities of the different currencies?
5. How do economic announcements and news affect prices?
6. Which indicators should you watch for profit?

Currency prices move because of supply and demand. Understand that when the lines of supply and demand cross, the price is set for the money. There are a few ways currency rates can change.
- Equality in supply and demand
- An increase in supply, decrease in demand
- A decline in supply, increase in demand

When there is a demand increase, the rate will rise because the amount becomes lower. Prices will fall when the supply increases since the requests are more moderate. Prices will also fall when the demand decreases because the supply is higher. Conversely, when the supply decreases, the price increases.

If you can understand the concept of supply and demand, then you can understand how currency prices will change. Five factors influence supply and demand.
1. Trade flows
2. Investment flows
3. Money supply
4. Government intervention
5. Investor fear

Trade flow is when money is exchanged due to trade. There may be foreign demand for domestic products or national demand for foreign goods. A country may have a higher demand for foreign goods, so a country brings in the products, creating a trade deficit with the international company. When there is a demand by a foreign business for goods, there is a trade surplus.

There is a theory—the balance of payments—stating when a country has a surplus it becomes stronger; however, if there is a trade deficit it is weaker. Investment flow means countries are interested or not interested in bringing their money to another country. If a company desires an asset, in a foreign country, the domestic currency for that country increases, but the enterprise's money decreases in value due to an increase in supply.

Watching investment flows is harder than trade flows. Not all companies will show their hand with investments, and some countries do not have an accurate way to show deals. The missing information can lead you to make a critical error in judgment.

The government's treasury or central bank dictates money flow. A country may increase the supply of their currency for various reasons; however, when more money is in circulation it lowers the value. To monitor money supply, you will watch interest rates, quantitative easing, and government intervention. Quantitative easing it when the money supply increases to decrease interest rates to help securities cover debt obligations. US Treasuries, mortgage-backed securities, and collateralized debt obligations may be purchased by the central bank to help inflation, interest rates, and economic stability. For the bank to make a purchase, they need money, which means they create it.

Governments can intercede when there is an economic worry. Some governments interfere more than others in the setting of interest rates, currency rates, and inflation. Governments tend to intervene when there is a concern that the currency is too strong, too weak, or they are pegging it against another currency.
Hong Kong, China, Denmark, and Saudi Arabia peg their currency against another. The endeavor is to help keep stability in the financial market. However, pegging requires consistent intervention and manipulation to ensure the prices remain stable.

Investor fear, meaning fear the retail trader has, can impact the market. If traders fear market movements, they pull out, they put their money in safe havens, and stop trading for a time. Safe-haven currencies are perceived as protected. In times of trouble, investors buy USD because the US Treasury is thought to deal well with financial crises. The Swiss franc (CHF) is a safe-haven currency because gold backs their money. The Japanese yen is also seen as better in times of financial upheaval because Japan has a small amount of debt. Most of the debt in Japan is not in government accounts but individual Japanese investor accounts.

Before ending the talk on fundamental analysis, you should understand who the players are. Hedgers, manipulators, speculators, and facilitators affect the market. Hedgers try to reduce their risk and think the forex market is the place to limit their exposure. International business transactions are risky, but the risk can be offset with the right set up. Manipulators are central banks and other players who get into the market to influence the rates. Speculators are looking for risk as a means of making a profit, so they are the opposite of hedgers. You are a speculator. Facilitators are participants, who help hedgers, manipulators, and speculators place their trades. Facilitators are the brokers, dealers, and banks.

Remember when you read that the forex market is decentralized? All countries have a central bank, which sets rates for the big players—major banks. The leading banks like Bank of America, Bank of Montreal, and Goldman Sachs set currency rates for smaller banks, over the counter exchanges, and prime brokers.

Prime brokers can also help with client transactions. Customers can seek an executing dealer, who works with a prime broker. When you use a dealer, broker, or bank to place a trade electronically, the rate provides a profit for the facilitator. The major bank makes a profit, and so does the central bank. The profit is via pips. The reason different dealers and brokers do not have the same rates is that of the pips, which is also where you make your money.

Technical Analysis

Technical analysis works off of history. The history of price movements shows a pattern. Sometimes these patterns are not there. Trader psychology makes you think you see a pattern because you want to make a profit. However, in most instances, there are patterns. Patterns will vary, but two patterns are easier to spot than others. Beginners should concentrate on those patterns to develop strategies, and work towards learning more sophisticated analysis.

The idea is if you can find a pattern in historical price movements, you can predict the future. Unfortunately, there are numerous factors at play, as you discovered in the fundamental analysis.

Strategy for Going Forward

Investing your hard earned capital right now is dangerous. You could end up with significant losses unless you are a more intermediate forex trader. Of course, you may be reading through this because you are losing after several years of investing in forex. No matter who you are, there is something to learn from this strategy.

- Start a paper money account
- Get to know the currencies and the major pairs
- Study technical charts for patterns
- Use your paper money account to set up trade plans
- Record these fake trades in a journal
- Analyze your mistakes: where you too emotional, did you read the pattern wrong, did you miss the global picture? What can you do better?
- Repeat the above, continuing to learn better methods for trading, and increase the level of difficulty in your technical analysis to develop better strategies

You can succeed in forex trades, as long as you understand the global picture. Assessing the global picture and narrowing your trading strategy to a point in time, will help you profit.

CHAPTER 4
Getting to Know the Currencies

Currency rates move due to twelve factors:
1. What does the country's economy export?
2. Does the economy have a trade surplus or deficit?
3. Where does the country export?
4. What does country import?
5. Which country sends the imports?
6. Is the government debt market attractive?
7. Does the country have a decent equities market?
8. Is the government overinvolved?
9. Does the central bank interfere often, and have plenty of gold and currency reserves?
10. Is the country currency a safe-haven?
11. What economic announcements influence market rates?
12. How can you trade the money?

You should know the answer to all twelve questions for any monetary unit you are going to trade. In this chapter, the strategy is getting to understand the major currencies. When you know the major pairs, you will have at least seven ways to trade depending on the market for the day.

The Major USD Pairs
- EUR
- JPY
- GBP
- CHF
- AUD
- CAD
- NZD

The G7 countries include many who use the euro and are so named because they have a stable economy and financial situation compared to other nations. The list expanded to G20 countries as more places around the world increase in their stability. Investments have proven lucrative for places, such as Qatar, China, South Korea, and certain South American locations.

But, for now, you should know about eight currencies, the seven listed and the USD. Major currency pairs all have the US dollar in the pair. The International Standardization Organization or ISO has a code for listing these monetary units and their rates. Market traders assigned nicknames to five of the seven pairs.

The pairs are written as follows:
- EUR/USD
- GBP/USD
- AUD/USD
- NZD/USD
- USD/JPY
- USD/CHF
- USD/CAD

Notice for four of the seven pairs, the USD is the quote or counter currency. The position of the USD will matter to you later when you are trying to determine profit for your trading plan.

US Dollar Answers

To avoid repeating the questions, the replies to the questions above are here:
1. The USA has a trade deficit.
2. The US exports manufactured goods and other commercial services, with little agricultural products, fuels and mining products, travel and transportation in the mix.
3. Exports are sent primarily to the European Union, with Canada, Mexico, China, and Japan as trading partners.
4. The US imports manufactured products and other commercial services, as well as a high number of transportation and travel services, with a few agricultural and fuel/mining products brought in from other countries.
5. China is the first importer, with the European Union, Canada, Mexico, and Japan as importers to the USA.
    a. Moody's rates the debt market. The USA rating is Aaa but can change if the debt market worsens.

6. The US government does not get overly involved in the forex market; however, there are times it has intervened.
    a. The equities market brings investors to the country.
    b. The central bank has significant reserves to help keep the financial market stable.
    c. Important announcements include federal funds rate, nonfarm payrolls, unemployment, consumer price index, producer price index, trade balance, GDP (gross domestic product), Treasury international capital data. Other reports are durable goods orders, consumer confidence index, consumer sentiment index, factory orders, retail sales, manufacturing business survey, existing home sales, housing starts/building permits, new home sales, and the Standard and Poor's index.
    d. The USA is a safe-haven currency.
    e. The USD is available for trade on the spot forex market, forex futures, exchange traded funds, exchange traded notes, exchange traded forex options, and spot forex options.

So, how is this going to compare to other currencies in the major pairs?

The Euro

The Euro is a hard currency to assess because it is tied to more than eleven countries, with discussions of more countries adopting the euro or going back to their old currency. The countries using the euro include:

1. Spain
2. Austria
3. Portugal
4. Belgium
5. Netherlands
6. Finland
7. Luxembourg
8. France
9. Italy
10. Germany
11. Ireland

There are rules for countries to use the euro if this regulation is maintained a country can use the euro. In fact, after 1999, more countries started using the euro. Slovenia, Greece, Malta, Slovakia, Cyprus, and Estonia use the euro. Monaco, Montenegro, Vatican City, and San Marino also take the euro but do not belong to the Eurozone, which is the entity regulating inflation, deficits, currency stability, and interest rates.

Germany, Italy, France, and Spain are the most influential countries to assess the economic outlook for the Eurozone. Germany and Italy run a trade surplus, while France and Spain have a deficit. Germany and France export the majority of goods, where manufactured products are the highest percentage of exports. Italy comes in third regarding export income but is the second largest country to export manufactured goods. Germany, France, and Italy export mainly to the European Union, with the USA as a secondary importer of European goods. China, Switzerland, and the Russian Federation also import from Germany, France, and Italy.

The top three countries we are focusing on, import manufactured services and other commercial services the most. The European Union is also the top import partner. China, the United States, Switzerland, Russian Federation, and Libyan Arab Jamahiriya are also import partners with Germany, Italy, and France.

The debt market is not unified, so Moody provides a cumulative rating by looking at all the countries in the Eurozone. The rating is Aaa. The six largest equities markets are part of the Eurozone, which also helps provide the euro with an attractive equities market.

The European Central Bank oversees the euro. Its primary goal is to keep inflation below 2 percent. The combination of reserves at the ECB makes it one of the biggest currency reserves and gold deposits.
The ECB is known for its intervention, much like the European Union gets involved in the economic trade.

When you assess euro reports, you want to look at the ECB bid rate, trade balance, GDP, German unemployment, German industrial production, German ZEW, CPI flash estimate, German consumer price index, and German IFO.

The euro is not considered a safe-haven currency because there are too many players in the game. With so many countries using the euro and tying their economic data to reports, it is easy for the rates to change suddenly, without proper stability. You can trade the euro in the spot forex market, forex futures, ETFs, ETNs, exchange trade forex options, and spot forex options.

Canadian Dollar

The CAD or Canadian dollar is known as the *loonie*. Canada runs a trade deficit. Like most countries, manufactured goods and other commercial services are the main exports to the United States, European Union, China, Japan, and Mexico. Canada imports manufactured goods and other business services too, with the United States as the primary country they make trades with, but they also import from Mexico, Japan, China, and the European Union.

Like the previous two nations, Canada has an Aaa rating, an attractive equities market, and decent reserves. The government is not known to interfere. You will want to find out when reports come out for the Bank of Canada rates, as well as employment change, unemployment, CPI, PPI, GDP, foreign securities purchases, and trade balance.

The CAD is not a safe-haven. You can trade it in the same markets as the euro, but the spot market is most important to you.

The Pound Sterling

Better known in the forex world as GBP, the Great British Pound or Sterling, is the currency of the UK. It has a trade deficit with manufactured goods and commercial services as the main exports to the European Union, United States, China, Switzerland, and Canada. They import just as many of the same category of products to the above countries, except some of the imports come from Norway instead of Switzerland.

They Moody rating is the same as the other three major currencies, and their equities market is the fifth largest in the world. The Bank of England has reserves on par with the other countries in this discussion.
The government rarely gets involved in the forex market.

You should know when the Bank of England releases its rates. You also need to find out when the unemployment, CPI, PPI, GDP, trade balance, retail sales, PMI, and Halifax House Index reports are available.

The GBP is not a safe-haven currency. You can trade it like the CAD and EUR.

The Swiss Franc, CHF

The Swiss Franc (CHF) is a safe-haven currency, which can be traded in spot forex markets, as well as others mentioned above. Switzerland has a trade surplus with similar goods and services exported to the European Union, United States, Japan, China, and Hong Kong. Switzerland imports machinery, vehicles, metals, textiles, chemicals, and agricultural products from the EU, US, China, Japan, and Vietnam.

As with the other top countries, their rating is Aaa, with the 12th largest equities market and extremely high currency reserves and gold deposits. The Swiss government may occasionally intervene to maintain the Franc.

You want to pay attention to interest rate, KOF economic barometer, retail sales, inflation, employment, GDP, and trade balance reports.

Japanese Yen

Japan has always maintained low-interest rates and has the second largest surplus in the world. Japan exports motor vehicles, electronics, machinery, chemicals, and transport equipment to China, the US, EU, Korea, and Taiwan. It imports fuel, food, chemicals, and raw materials from China, the US, EU, Australia, and Saudi Arabia.

Japan as with all other currencies in this category has an Aaa rating from Moody and an attractive equities market. It also has one of the highest reserves in the world. The Bank of Japan and Ministry of Finance do intervene in the forex market, which may be one of the reasons the economy is so stable. You will need to track the Bank of Japan call rate, Tankan Manufacturing Index, GDP,

Tokyo CPI, and trade balance reports. Also, keep an ear out for any rumors of the government interventions that occasionally happen so that you can be prepared for changes. The Yen is a safe-haven currency because of the reserves and large domestic investors, who own the Japanese government debt. You can trade the Yen on the spot market, ETFs, ETNs, and options markets.

Australian Dollar

Australia is the 12th largest country in the world with a trade deficit. Australia exports iron, coal, gold, meat, ore, wool, wheat, and machinery. Most of their exports head to China, but Japan, the EU, South Korea, and India also import Australia's goods. Australia imports from the EU, China, US, Thailand, and Japan. They bring in machinery, transport, and telecommunication equipment, as well as computers, office machines, and petroleum products.

The equities market is attractive, and so is their debt rating of Aaa. Australia has smaller reserves than other countries, and the government is not overly aggressive in their interference.

Watch for the Reserve Bank of Australia, employment, unemployment, CPI, trade balance, GDP, PPI, retail sales, and commodity price reports. The AUD is not a safe-haven currency, and you can trade it in the spot market.

New Zealand Dollar

The NZD or Kiwi is a commodity currency because the economy depends on commodity exports. They have a trade deficit. New Zealand exports dairy products, wood, fish, meat, and machinery to Australia, EU, US, China, and Japan.
The country imports machinery, vehicles, aircraft, electronics, textiles, plastics, and petroleum from Australia, the EU, China, US, and Japan. As with the other seven currencies, the Moody rating is Aaa. The equities market is not large, but

it is attractive to investors. The reserve bank does not have gold deposits but keeps a few million in currency reserves.

New Zealand's government rarely interferes. You should watch for the Reserve Bank of New Zealand rates, employment, CPI, GDP, retail sales, trade balance, economic research report, and business confidence report.

New Zealand is not a safe-haven for money, and you can trade it in the spot forex market, futures, ETFs, and options markets.

Already you have a lot of information about the major currency pairs, and you probably feel overwhelmed. How are you supposed to remember everything? How will it matter? You know it matters because economic and government data determines how the currencies will change in strength. More importantly, you need to know the information so you can assess how one currency will be moving against another. How will economic reports impact the NZD and USD? Will the USD gain strength after individual reports are released? The answer is yes.

Strategy for this Chapter

Learning the information above is imperative. However, you will also need to set up an economic reports calendar for the top seven currencies. There are calendars online, but you can create your alerts to tell you when each countries reports will release in the media.

Experts on trading channels like CNBC will mention when reports are about to come out. The reason for that is to help traders understand technical patterns they see and why those patterns may change, along with helping fundamental traders make a profit.

You can trade on information when reports are due:
- Expected results
- Actual results
- Market sentiment regarding the results

You may decide to place a trade on market sentiment, where there is a suspicion of an increase or decrease in a currency pair based on expected results. For example, if someone says the unemployment report is an improvement over the last one, people might start to invest in the currency for that country with the expectation that there will be an increase in value. Some players will stay out of the market until the actual results are released.

They will then jump in with a trade based on the news. If the real results mirrored the expected results, more traders would get into the market. If the results were worse than expected, some will fear the outcome, and stay out of the market. You can follow the herd on the actual results to make a profit or wait till they jump out with their profit and ride the return to normalcy. A standard rate is one that is not influenced by traders and results for the day. It is where the rate will remain for a while until something else causes it to increase or decrease.

Start out by learning when the reports are due. Next, watch what happens with the expected and actual results. How did the market move? Where traders fearful of investing before the report and then providing profitable moves afterward? You are going to learn to read the market and the traders in the market.

It is in your best interest to know all the components of forex before you begin investing your money. Too many people get into the market without a true understanding of how it works and the factors that influence currency prices. The fundamental trading analysis is information. The new details come out on specific dates, and you want to know when that will happen. You want to watch the news to find out what is going on in the world. Each day should start with the news, whether you get it via internet or TV. See what is happening because the news can cause a shift in how people will trade.

Market fear is one thing you need to be cautious of; particularly, when it can affect trends. Terrorism or huge news that shakes the world of any sort is going to cause investors to run to the safe-haven currencies until things calm down. Presidential elections can have an effect on a countries currency strength. Bear these factors in mind when you think about your trading plan.

Your strategy should be to learn the currency information for each of the major seven pairs, to wake up to the news, and then to look for technical trends.

CHAPTER 5

Technical Charts

Technical charts are available via your dealer, broker, or Google. You need to be cautious about where you pull your information because some places can give you old data to track. For example, Google pulls information quickly, but it is not for trading. You are better off going with charts on your trading platform.

You know that the information is reliable and people are trading on it.

What are Technical Charts?

Technical charts are historical data plotted for you to see. The time frame of a graph is set up by you but has limitations. Most charts have data for the last hour up to the previous five years. It is possible to search for data from ten years ago if you want to. However, ten years is a long span of time without a clear trend to help you trade today. Five years ago is important because of the financial crisis. You can see how currencies reacted during a time of turmoil when many countries suffered a mortgage crisis. You could look at ten years ago to see what happened before the subprime mortgage crisis occurred. But, these trends will not remain. There is too much going on in the market to keep the same patterns.

At most from older charts, you can look at what happened and what to avoid in times of a crisis from graphs that offer data that is five years or older.

Types of Charts

There are three types of graphs. The first is a line diagram. The line chart shows plotted points at specific intervals throughout a set time frame. The line will either go up or down on the data points. For a graph, the time is at the bottom or the X axis. The Y axis is the price or quote for the currency pair. On the chart, the quote currency price is set because the base currency is always one.

If you see a graph, with a line going from 1.0456 to 1.0556, this is an uptrend with the quote currency becoming weaker against the base currency. A downtrend would show the price going from 1.0556 to1.0356.

The second type of chart is a bar graph. Bar charts are perfect for you to draw trend lines, to measure retracement levels, or to see the average price volatility of a currency pair. Each bar will show a trading range for a period. The larger a bar on the graph, the greater the trading range. The larger bar can also represent more volatility in the market.

Candlestick charts are named for the bar representation that has a "wick" on both ends. The "wicks" are the lower and upper tail. The bottom of the candle is the open price, and the top of the box is the closing price for the day. The body is the length of the rectangular shape. Candlesticks are white or black in color depending on whether the closing price was lower than the opening price. In fact, on a darker shaded candlestick, the close will be on the bottom of the candlestick, with the open at the top.

Reading a Chart

Reading charts is simple or complicated, depending on the type of chart you use. A line chart is the most basic because you see plotted points with a line going through them. Bars and candlesticks are harder to read because you need to understand the anatomy of the depictions. There will be more on candlesticks in a later chapter. For now, know that you will want to spend time learning how to read the charts. You are reading the charts to look for trends.

Searching for Trends

Technical traders believe there are chart formations; you can use to predict the future price of a currency pair. Basic chart formations are reversal patterns, where a pattern shows the current price movement will come to an end.
If the trend is in an upswing, a reversal is a downturn.
Continuation patterns show a pause in a directional price move, where a back and forth movement occurs before the first trend continues.

Other trends are:
- Double tops
- Double bottoms
- Head and shoulders
- Inverted head and shoulders
- Flags
- Triangles (symmetrical and ascending)
- Descending triangles
- Doji
- Hammer and shooting stars
- Spinning tops
- Engulfing lines
- Tweezers Tops and Bottoms

Your head might be spinning a little right now. If you are a beginner in forex, you probably have not studied these trends in-depth. You do not have to know every pattern. You want to start with a strategy that makes the entry and exit of your trading plan easy for you.
You should not get lost in the more complicated trends until you learn to recognize the fundamental patterns.

Strategy for Technical Charts

Start with a graph you can easily read, something that is familiar. Look for patterns. You can find figures that represent the patterns listed above. See if you can spot the various trends, such as an area on the chart that looks like it went up, then down before going up a little higher, and repeating the first up/down trend before the second higher peak. This is a head and shoulder because you have two peaks that are about the same height, with a higher peak in the middle.

Your strategy, for right now, is to learn to read trends to recognize potential trends. Later, you can start to develop a trading plan involving the meanings of these patterns.

CHAPTER 6
Support and Resistance Trends

Support and resistance patterns are a type of continuation trend, where you have a consistent reversal and continuation. Typically, support and resistance trend is part of a larger overall trend, but you narrow the information to a time frame when you can invest.

For example, you might see an uptrend on the EUR/USD for the last week. However, when you narrow the time frame to an hour, the pair keeps going to a particular rate before it reverses to a point before it goes back to the uptrend.

Without numbers, it is difficult to see the trend. Let's say the EUR/USD opens at 1.0456. After an hour, the pair reaches 1.0556. It returns to 1.0460 in 10 minutes. In 40 minutes, the price is near 1.0560. For four hours, the pair continued fluctuating from 1.0456 to 1.0560. After four hours, the pair took off breaking out of the up and down trend pattern to reach 1.0660.

The reason this type of pattern is a support and resistance trend, although it is also a continuation with reversals, is because there is a line the price does not cross when it is in an uptrend and one it will not pass when it turns into a downtrend.

The support line for this trend is drawn on the graph to indicate a point when the currency rate does not go below a certain amount. For example, let's say the price will not go below 1.0460, so the support line is drawn at the bottom of the peak that forms each time the pattern goes from a downtrend to an uptrend.

The resistance line is drawn where the pattern reverses from an uptrend into a downtrend. A new peak will form. The line is set at 1.0659 for our example. As a trader, you can strategize how to take advantage of the up and down trends. It will be a matter of when you enter the market.

If you know the currency rate will return to near 1.0460, you can set a trade in motion to buy the EUR/USD at 1.0464. You know the trend will turn around near 1.0660. You decide you want to sell when you earn 100 pips, instead of trying to obtain 200 pips profit. You sell out at 1.0560, instead of riding the trend to 1.0660.

You made 100 pips profit, which is $100. For currency pairs with the USD as the quote currency, the value of a single pip on a standard lot of 10,000 is $1. If your lot size is 100,000, then your profit is $10 per pip; therefore, $1,000 for a trade where you make 100 pips.

The best part about the support and resistance trend is knowing the low and high of the currency rate for as long as the trend continues. The pattern may occur multiple times in ten minutes or repeat a few times in four hours.

To trade on this trend, you need to see it on the chart, recognize the correct pattern, and watch for a few minutes before you set up your trade. If you jump in without knowing the proper pattern for the time frame, you could end up with a loss.

How to Use the Trend

You use the pattern by recognizing it. Here are some steps.
- Assess a currency pair chart for 30 days of rates.
- Decide what the overall trend has been in that month's time.
- Shrink the time frame to the current week, what do you notice? Is the pattern different, does it seem like there is an overall uptrend, but the last week has been a downtrend?
- Now, shrink the time frame to the day you want to trade. Has the pattern changed? Is there support and resistance trend or a clear up or down trend?
- If you see support and resistance trend, watch how the pattern behaves. You should be able to see a history of the pattern of the support line and resistance line.
- Choose an entry point.
- Set a stop loss.
- Set your exit point.
- Repeat as long as the trend remains valid.

You can also decide to stay in a trend if it is doing you a favor and continuing towards a higher profit. The stop loss or trailing stop loss ensures you make a profit as long as the price does not reverse.

The support and resistance trend is a good one to look for when you are a beginner because it is often the clearest pattern on a graph. Once you understand how to read up and down trends to make the most of the profit, you can move on to other trends.

CHAPTER 7
Breakout Trends

Breakout trends are a continuation of a trend that is no longer stopped by the support or resistance line.
There are indicators on the charts that will show when a breakout may occur. Typically, the reversal of a different trend is shorter, with a quick return to the original pattern. For example, if the price was 1.0460 for the support line, but the last time a downtrend occurred, the price was 1.0560, before the reversal to 1.0660, and the next time the rate went down to 1.0599, before going past 1.0660, there is a potential breakout trend.

When a breakout trend occurs, you ideally want to be in a trade already. You want to have your position chosen to take advantage of the breakout from the support or resistance line. In this position, your stop loss or trailing stop loss is not activated, so your position does not close early. You can set a taking profit order, which pulls out the amount you made from the current trend and leaves the capital to earn money on the breakout pattern.

How to Use a Breakout Trend

If you can see the indicators, you can set an entry point to get in before the breakout occurs. There are different signs, which are not explored in this chapter. You will learn about them in a later chapter.
For now, understand that you can look for indicators that will help you see a breakout trend. Find the pattern. Watch for a few minutes and then place an order.

Set your stop loss as a trailing stop loss, so you follow the currency rate changes. A stop loss shall be fixed at a price, while a trailing stop loss is set for a pip distance. If you buy the EUR/USD at 1.0460 and you set a stop loss at 1.0450, the trade is closed when 1.0450 is reached. If you use a trailing stop, at 1.0450 and the price increases to 1.0470, the trailing stop loss moves to 1.0460. If the breakout trend does not occur, the position is closed, without significant loss to your capital.
If the breakout pattern happens, you will gain as long as the position remains open and going in your favor. The trailing stop loss will close the position when

a reversal occurs. You also have the taking profit order to save the profit you made before a reversal happens and you lose a little of the money you gained.

The breakout trend is another strategy for beginners because you should have a position open on a support and resistance trend, allowing you to make a better profit if a breakout pattern occurs. You know you can grab your profit, and keep your capital earning money.

CHAPTER 8
Candlestick Charts

Candlestick charts are more complicated than line graphs because you have to assess the light and dark shades of the candles to determine the pattern. A formation may exist, but if you cannot understand what the light and dark mean on the chart, you will have trouble creating a strategy.
Start by looking at candlestick charts that have formations depicted for you.

There are plenty of charts online that you can study. Just see if you can pick out certain things like two peaks that are on the bottom of the graph. For example, a price might increase, but there are times when two peaks form on a reversal before the pattern continues in an uptrend. Look for flags, head and shoulders, and triangle formations.

These occur based on the lines drawn on the charts. Eventually, you can draw your lines, but for now, use your broker or dealers charting software to see the indicators.
If you see patterns like a reversal pattern, doji, or continuation pattern, you know to set a trade. Doji patterns indicate indecision by traders in the market. Reversal patterns show an end to one trend and a beginner of a new trend in the opposite direction. Continuation patterns are a continued trend in the same direction, even if there are minor starts and stops.

Reading candlesticks is about seeing the lines, but understanding one complete candlestick is for a particular time. Most charts offer a day's worth of information in one candlestick drawn on the graph. However, sometimes you can limit the candlestick chart to minutes or hours.

An Explanation of Trends

Double Tops or Bottoms: this is a formation that will indicate a reversal of the current trend. The double tops will form in an uptrend to show a downtrend is coming, while the double bottoms form to show an uptrend is pending.
Head and shoulders and inverted IIS are triple tops or bottoms, where a reversal in trend is also indicated. In this instance, the three peaks were failed attempts to continue the pattern, and thus a reversal in trend occurs.

Flags are consolidation patterns. Typically, flags form in a counter-trend direction, where the trend will continue, often in a breakout, so there is value there. You spot flags by drawing the support and resistance lines, and a pole that will come from the continued overall pattern.

Triangles can appear in ascending, descending, or symmetrical shapes. Symmetrical triangles form on a downward slope for the upper edges and an upward slope for the lower edges, where a triangle appears.
Symmetrical triangles do not indicate which way a breakout trend will occur, just that one may occur, or the trend can resume.
However, if you have different triangles, along with a symmetrical triangle you can usually learn which direction the pattern will go towards as a way to invest correctly.

Strategy for Candlesticks

- Learn to spot trends.
- Create an entry point based on the indicators that a new trend or continuing trend is occurring.
- Set your stop loss, trailing stop loss, or taking profit order.
- Exit the trade.
- Test your theory with a paper money account first, to determine if you see the proper trends and able to make a profit off of the concept.

Chapter 9
Risk Management and Order Protection

Entering a trade takes thought. You do not look at a pattern and try someone else's strategy in the hopes that you will become a millionaire. Instead, you decide what is right for you based on your situation.

You have capital to invest. What is this capital? Where did the money come from for you to use? You earned this money. You worked long hours, spent time away from your kids, or maybe you were given the money through an inheritance. Most of us work very hard for the money we make and do not want to lose it quickly.

We have plans for what we want to use the money to buy. We also know that securing a better retirement, investing to get extra funds for a vacation, and increasing our emergency fund are all good purposes for our money. But, to risk these funds on a whim could create more trouble than it is worth.

Why set yourself up for heartache? You should not, and the strategies in the previous chapters help you see where you need to learn more or stick to basics until you have mastered them.

This chapter is about risk management, top mistakes, and orders you can use to protect your investment strategy.

Risk management examines your risk aversion level and helps you set orders to protect your position. You develop strategies based on the amount of money you are willing to lose per trade.

Yes, there will come a time when money is lost. As stated in trading psychology, you have to accept that loss will occur. It is what you do to ensure a smaller loss occurs next time or not at all that will determine if your risk management strategies are paying off.

The Percent Rule

Many traders develop a risk management plan based on a percentage. If they have $1,000 to invest per trade, they will determine how much of that $1,000

they are willing to lose in that plan. One percent loss of $1,000 is $10. You could always lose on a trade if you set a stop loss order at one percent. Why? Your stop loss will be too tight to the currency rate for you to make a profit. A tight stop loss can be activated before you are ready.
It is still okay to use the percent rule. Many traders find it is successful if only to keep their emotions in check. There is a better rule to follow.

Profit Taking

You can devise a strategy based on profit, where you minimize the risk. This strategy is when you use a basic trend like support and resistance and maximize the potential earnings. You already know the caps for the up and down trend, so you can predict a steady profit for as long as the trend is repeated.

In fact, you can hunt for the support and resistance trend in any of the G20 currency pairs on a daily basis to ensure you will make a profit.
If you know the potential profit is 100 pips because the currency rate will change by 100 pips, you can set your stop loss to take a profit. Instead of setting the stop loss right at 100 pips, you will set it to earn 90 pips. You still earn money, but you do not risk loss.

What happens if 100 pips are not realized, and only 95 pips are gained? If you set your exit strategy at 90, you do not care. If you wanted 100 pips profit, then you potentially lost the entire earnings of that trade due to a stop loss error.

You do not want to leave yourself open for losses when you can use a basic strategy to maximize your profit.
There are three levels of risk aversion: low, medium, and high. Someone with high-risk aversion will not take risks. They will practice strategies that ensure a minimum return on their investment each time, but typically earn a steady, small profit. A low-risk aversion means the person is not averse to risk and will set up trades with more risk in the hope of gaining a quicker, larger profit.
You can set up all three types of trades based on different strategies. For example, you might increase your risk on a support and resistance trend, have a medium risk on a breakout trend, and lower your risk on a new type of trend strategy like using candlestick charts to predict the price movement.

Most investors want to have the same risk management for each trade to avoid losses. It is better to stay with a certain risk aversion level because you will turn a steady profit over time.

Calculating Profit

Potential profit can be calculated prior to entering a trade. This helps you set your stop loss or another type of order to protect your capital.
All currency pairs with USD as the quote currency have a set pip value based on the lot sizes.

1,000 lot sizes equal $0.01 per pip
10,000 lot sizes= $1 per pip
100,000 lot sizes are $10 per pip

Lot sizes are also the same in USD required to open a trade, so 1,000 lot size will cost $1,000 to enter. If you use 10,000 lot sizes, you spend $10,000 for one lot. If you gain 1 pip with a lot size of 1,000 you will make $0.01 per pip. A hundred pip movement on a lot size of $10,000 is $100, but only $10 for 1,000 lot sizes. It may not look like a huge profit depending on the lot size; however, if you remember multiple trades over time with little loss, and mostly gains, then you can understand how to make a profit.

You make a profit by making sure nearly 100% of your trades are profitable. Traders who work on the profit calculation to enter a trade, tend to be more successful because they are looking at how much is being made and not at the loss. Sometimes positive thinking really is powerful.

Setting Orders

Stop Loss: this is the most common type of order that protects your position. After you enter the market with a market or limit order, you need to set a type of stop loss. The simple stop loss is set at a price point, such as 1.0456 and it will not move. If the currency rate hits 1.0456 your position is closed. If it skips over that and goes below 1.0456, you are guaranteed a close at 1.0456 with most dealers.

Trailing stop loss: a stop loss that trails is one that follows the price increase by a set pip differential. If you enter at 1.0456 and set a trailing stop loss 20 pips off the price, you will follow the currency rate as it increases. If the price goes to 1.0476, your trailing stop loss rises to 10.0456. If the rate turns around and goes below the last point of the trailing stop loss, the position closes and you keep the profit at the 20 pips price or whatever the difference is between the open price and where you set the trailing stop loss.

Taking Profit: a taking profit order allows you to keep your capital in play. The order is still open; however, you remove the profit you have made thus far during the trade. For example, if you earned 100 pips, you can close out a part of your trade to remove the $100 you made on the 10,000 lot size. The capital remains in until another order is activated, such as a stop loss or you close the position.

You want to use these orders to protect your position; especially, if you are not at the computer during the trading day. Many traders set up an opening trade, but cannot monitor it, and hope their stop loss or taking profit closes the position for a profitable trade.

Ten Mistakes to Avoid

Part of your strategy is to avoid common mistakes. Here are ten mistakes traders have made that you should not make.

1. Do not use indicators or fancy trading tools until you understand how price movements occur both from a technical and fundamental standpoint. Indicators have their uses, but only after you understand price action.

2. You should view each trade from a risk reward standpoint. If you cannot keep your risk at the appropriate aversion level, do not invest in the market. Wait

until there is a trade that fits your strategy. Additionally, look at the reward for the risk you are taking. Is there enough profit to be made for the risk you have? If you need to increase your lot size to a million by using leverage, but have to sell your home, empty your child's college savings, or otherwise use money you do not want to invest, the reward is not worth it.

3. Traders who begin without an understanding of position sizing will lose. Position sizing helps you determine where to set the stop loss. You should not adjust your stop loss to meet the lot sizes you want to trade, but rather adjust your position size to meet the stop loss distance. This concept is about a tight stop loss. You can reduce the size of your position to extend the stop loss, without increasing the potential loss. However, if you increase the lot size, you still need to keep the stop loss tight to avoid a larger loss.

4. Some traders gamble by putting their emotions in the trade. You need to be responsible with your trades and avoid the greed/depression cycle that comes with gambling.

5. Many intermediate traders still fail to use a trading plan. Do not be this person. As a basic or intermediate trader, have a plan for entering the market, protecting your position, and closing the trade.

6. Use discipline. When you have a strategy and trading plan in motion, do not change it. You might be tempted to do so, but do not. Stick to the plan. Yes, if you see a significant loss because of a mistake, close the position, but otherwise, do not play with the stop loss for fear of losing your capital. Let it ride.

7. Patience is a virtue. There is a reason the phrase is a cliché—it is true. Patience ensures you wait to enter the market when there is a position to make a profit from, as well as maintaining your trading plan to avoid mistakes.

8. Traders who fail to look at a wider time frame and trade only on four hours of information will lose. You cannot see how a pattern is forming with accuracy if you ignore the global picture. If you want to trade for 15 minutes, great, do that but do not forget to see what has happened for the day, and then for the last hour. Missing a pattern will ensure you lose money.

9. Traders who do not take profits out and continue for a larger profit, make a huge mistake. There is a potential to lose everything including your capital. Do

not let this happen. Take your profit and remain in the trade with protection orders in place.

10. Do not over trade. There are times when there is not an investment. The volatility is low, the volume is low, and traders fear the losses. Do not hunt for something that is not there. As a bonus tip, when you develop a strategy make sure you have the right dealer. Some brokers charge more than five pips as a spread. The pip spread is the difference between the buy and sell price for the currency pair. This price can be five pips, but some dealers charge more. Assess dealers, learn who is reputable, and then start to trade.

CONCLUSION

Thank for making it through to the end of *Forex Trading: Proven Techniques for Maximum Profit*. Let's hope it was informative and able to provide you with all of the tools you need to achieve your goals of making money in the forex market.

The next step is to take what you have learned, discover your trading style, and create a strategy that fits your capital, risk aversion, and time frame.
Only you can develop a plan that is going to work for you. No one else can provide a strategy to maintain maximum profit every time. Worse, if you are using a strategy that is for 1 million lot sizes and you cannot afford anything but a nano lot size, the strategy is not going to work for you.
Forex trading is like any other trading system, in that you need a plan based on your situation.

If you turn green at the thought of losing a million dollars on a trade, but another person has billions, you will not succeed.
As you learned in the chapters of this book, you can take the information provided, find out how it relates to you, and begin trading for success.

One way to trade for maximum profit is to avoid getting emotional, either too happy or too depressed to continue. Emotions will get in the way of your success every time. Treat forex as a business that needs to turn a profit, but will sustain some losses, and any strategy you design based on the time you have to buy/sell currencies, your risk aversion, and capital will ensure a profit more than a loss.

Remember to find an entry point. Set the time frame you will trade in based on the patterns you see. Set your stop loss orders. Exit the trade early if you see significant losses, but not due to panic.

You should not alter your trading plan once it is in motion unless your stop loss did not work and you see a greater loss than you wanted. Sometimes you have to let the trade play out and learn from your mistakes.
However, you can always minimize your losses if you are around to see the market turning against your position.
 The one thing you do not want to do is use a strategy, panic, and lose the profit you could have made. It happens more often than you might imagine.
Take what you have learned, use paper money trading accounts, and devise strategies from this book to fit your situation.

MEET THE AUTHOR

Oduse David Oluwadamilola is a prolific writer on a wide variety of topics ranging from Lifestyle, Business Tips, Politics, Economics and Finance, Sports, Relationship Tips, Food & Nutrition, Physical Fitness, and a lot more. He is the founder/CEO of ***Kings Media Limited:*** An online platform for sharing information that affects our general lives. You can join him on facebook by joining the facebook group; **Information Portal Worldwide.** He's also the admin of Kings Media Blog via https://www.kingmediablog.com You can contact him by email through odusedamilola@gmail.com for your writing services and content creation.

www.ingramcontent.com/pod-product-compliance
Lightning Source LLC
Chambersburg PA
CBHW082122220526

45472CB00009B/2273